"To be one, to be united is a great thing. But to respect the right to be different is maybe even greater."

BONO

"Come on Evie, come on Isla, it's bedtime! Which story would you like to hear tonight?"

"I want to hear the story of us,
What Makes Our Family Special."
Evie answered.

"Well, Gran Gran was born in Barbados, a small island in the Caribbean. And Grandad's parents are from Guyana, a country in South America."

"Mummy's parents were both born in Manchester, in England. Nanny's parents are from Ireland, and Grandad's parents are English."

"What is special about Ireland?" asked Isla.

"Let me tell you... Shall we go on an **adventure?**" asked Daddy.

"Yes, come on Caterpillar!"

"Yes!"

Did you know?

Ireland is approximately 367 miles away. We can travel there by boat or by plane. There is the Northern and the Republic of Ireland. Northern Ireland is part of the United Kingdom, whereas the Republic of Ireland is an independent nation.

Ireland has a lot of history and many traditions. One traditional saying is: "You have the luck of the Irish." Let's go to Ireland to find out why...

As Evie and Isla arrive, they bump into a man dressed all in green and wearing a tall hat. He was looking for something.

"Hey Mister! What are you looking for?" asked Isla.

"Hello, I'm Liam. I'm a leprechaun! You can call me Liam the Leprechaun. I'm looking for my pot of gold, I'm not certain where I've left it."

Did you know?

Irish legends tell of a type of fairy that stands about as tall as a three-year-old child and lives in the Irish countryside — this is a leprechaun. So, if you see a small, bearded-man wearing a green suit and hat, you may have just seen one!

"We can help you," said Evie, "where should we start to look?"

"Let's go to the Blarney Stone! If you kiss the stone, it gives luck. We'll need luck to find my pot of gold." said Liam the Leprechaun. "Right, off to Cork we go!"

Once at the Blarney Stone, Evie, Isla and Liam the Leprechaun **lean back**, holding the safety handles, and **kiss** the Blarney stone.

Once finished, a lady also visiting the Blarney Stone asked, "Why do you need **luck**?"

"We are looking for a **lost pot of gold!**" explained Isla.

"This won't help you find your pot of gold," replied the lady. "Kissing the Blarney Stone helps with the skill of **flattery** and **eloquence**... It doesn't give you luck."

"What does el-o-quence and flat-ter-y mean?" asked a puzzled Evie.

The passer-by explained, "It means to be good at **persuasion** and giving **praise**."

"Ok, so, what's next?" asked Evie.

"I know," said Liam the Leprechaun, "we have to find a **four-leaf clover** — they're lucky, you know."

Evie, Isla and Liam the Leprechaun looked around the fields
searching and searching and searching... until...

... Suddenly!
"I've found one.
Look! I have one!"
Evie shouted.

Did you know?
A shamrock is a young clover - both are symbols of Ireland.

Another passer-by asked why the trio needed **luck**.

"We are looking for a **lost pot of gold**," explained Evie.

"That won't help you find your pot of gold," the gentleman said, "although it is believed four-leaf clovers bring luck, and represent faith and hope... what you need is a rainbow!" he advised.

Did you know?
It is often said that Ireland is home to more four-leaf clovers than anywhere else in the world, giving meaning to the phrase "the luck of the Irish."

"Yes!" realised Liam the Leprechaun. "Of course that's where I left it. We must **hurry** before it gets **dark**."

"We need **rain** and **sunshine**," said Isla.

Evie, Isla and Liam the Leprechaun find a rock to wait on. All of a sudden, it started to rain; luckily, Evie and Isla had their **wellies**, **raincoat** and **umbrella**.

They all sat under the umbrella and **waited** and **waited** and **waited** for the rain to finally stop.

Suddenly the rain stopped, the sun came out and there it was... the biggest rainbow ever seen! They ran to the end of the rainbow, and there they found the big pot of gold!

"Thank you so much," said Liam the Leprechaun, "please take a piece of gold each as a **thank you**."

It was time for Evie and Isla to say their goodbyes.

"How was your trip to Ireland?" asked Daddy.

"It was so **beautiful!** We kissed the Blarney Stone..." Evie answered,

"...found a four leaf **clover** and followed a **rainbow** to find a leprechaun's pot of **gold!**" continued Isla.

"We are **proud** to be Irish," the sisters both said.

As Daddy turned off the lamp, he looked down at his smiling sleeping little ladies. He knew they were **dreaming** of their adventure in Ireland.

The next morning, Evie and Isla put on their coats and immediately felt something in their pockets.

It was their piece of gold from the leprechaun!

As they left their house to head to school, Evie said,
"Look Isla, under your foot."

"Oh wow, it's a £10 note!" said Isla.

A passing lady said, "Wow. You must have the luck of the Irish," winking at Evie and Isla.

Where is Ireland?

And where to next..?

Blue Stella Books
First Published in the UK in 2021 by Blue Stella owned by Danielle Clarke

Blue Stella
PO Box 2190
CROYDON
CR90 9UJ

www.bluestella.co.uk

Text Copyright © 2020 by Danielle Clarke
Illustrations Copyright © 2020 by Lily Carver

All rights reserved

ISBN 978-1-8382876-3-4

Written by Danielle Clarke
Edited by Kieran Simmonds
Printed in the UK

www.ingramcontent.com/pod-product-compliance
Lightning Source LLC
Chambersburg PA
CBHW042129040426
42450CB00002B/128